Unvarnished Truth
The Good, The Bad, and The Ugly of The Insurance Industry

Glen Nielsen

ISBN: 978-1-77277-033-9

PUBLISHED BY:
10-10-10 PUBLISHING
MARKHAM, ON
CANADA

Contents

DEDICATION

This book is dedicated to the source of my strength, my Lord and Savior, Jesus Christ.

"Not that I am speaking of being in need, for I have learned in whatever situation I am to be content. I know how to be brought low, and I know how to abound. In any and every circumstance, I have learned the secret of facing plenty and hunger, abundance and need. I can do all things through him who strengthens me."
– Phillipians 4:11-13 ESV

I would also like to dedicate this book to the memory of my dad, Ronald J. Nielsen. I will never forget our conversations that helped me grow into the man that God is refining.

FOREWORD

Glen has been in the industry for 10 years. He's seen a lot of bad things happen to good people like you. You might have thought that you have good coverage but Glen can tell you different.

The book, *Unvarnished Truth*, will give you many insights about the insurance industry. You will finally know what to look for in your policies. This book will clear up any confusion you might have had, and answer such questions as "What do I need?" "How can I tell what's covered in my policy?" "What does it really say/mean in the fine print of my policy?"

Read carefully what Glen presents in this very important book. Your future just might depend on it.

Raymond Aaron
NY Times Bestselling Author

ACKNOWLEDGEMENTS

Many people contributed to this book.

I would like to start by acknowledging Mike Bixler of US Health Advisors for his insights on what is going on with health insurance.

Sandy Nelson of Prairie State Impressions in Franklin Park, IL for sharing the perspective of insurance from a Human Resources Professional's point of view.

Raymond Aaron for creating the 10-10-10 program and his encouragement. And everyone at The Raymond Aaron Group for their support and encouragement. A special thank you to Liz Ventrella for her constant efforts, going above and beyond, returning phone calls, being patient with a first time author and insight as to how to make this finally happen, to Pavitra Phagoo, my Personal Book Architect, for guiding and helping me navigate the new-to-me arena of publishing, and to Carla Van Wees, Laura Dykstra, and Tory Johnston for always smiling, making Kelly and I feel welcome, and constantly encouraging me to be my best and reach for the stars.

Eddie Soto, owner of E.S. Online Enterprises, for his support and encouragement.

My mom, Therese Nielsen, for her love, encouragement and support. This book would not be possible without your help.

Brent and Kim Hager for encouragement and support throughout the book writing process.

My loving bride, Kelly. I couldn't have done this without your continued encouragement. Thank you for believing in me when other people deserted us.

ABOUT THE AUTHOR

Glen Nielsen has been in the insurance industry for ten years and was an educator prior to that. Glen's first series, Unvarnished Truth, capitalizes on his passion for helping people and educating the middle class (95%) on what the upper class (5%) knows. A native of Chicago, he now resides in the northern Chicago suburbs with his wife where he is a personal financial coach and business advisor to clients across the nation.

A NOTE TO THE READER

The information, including opinions and analysis, contained herein is based on the author's personal experience and is not intended to provide professional advice. The author and the publisher make no warranties, either expressed or implied, concerning the accuracy, applicability, effectiveness, reliability or suitability of the contents. If you wish to apply or follow the advice or recommendations mentioned herein, you take full responsibility for your actions. The author and publisher of this book shall in no event be held liable for any direct, indirect, incidental or consequential damages arising directly or indirectly from the use of any information contained in this book. All content is for information only and is not warranted for content accuracy or any other implied or explicit purpose.

Chapter 1
Introduction/Overview
"I need what?!"

I became a licensed insurance producer in February of 2006. Since then I've seen a lot of bad things happen to good people because they weren't properly educated about the world of insurance. That's the purpose of this book; to help educate you, the reader, so that you know what types of coverages there are and what to look out for in your policies, allowing you to make an educated decision as to what policies to get, what policies not to get, who to work with, who not to work with, what company to go with, etc. You have a lot of choices and if you make the wrong choice it could potentially hurt you and your family, financially speaking. My hope is that you will gain better insight into the insurance industry, learn a little bit about the different types of policies, the reasons why you should have insurance and the different types of insurance coverage that you need. It's about protecting not only yourself and your assets, but most importantly your family.

You may have heard of the poem "The Dash" that talks about how people may not remember when you were born, or when you die, but they will remember that little dash in between those days. This book is also about your dash. What is your dash all about? What is your life all about? How does insurance play into your dash, your life? And what kind of legacy you will leave behind? Are you going to leave a great legacy of "Wow, they really knew how to protect us!" or are you going to leave a legacy behind of "Wow, you know he really didn't protect us like he should have." The hope is that this may enlighten people that insurance is all about protecting your dash, more specifically your family. It's all about making sure that nothing happens to it.

I never really was interested in getting into the insurance and financial services industry to be totally honest. And most people would say the same thing. They never dreamed "Oh, one day I'm going to be in the financial services industry and be an advisor." Very, very rarely will you hear someone actually say this. It all happened by chance, if you will. I was an elementary P.E. teacher for 10 years and for some reason it just wasn't fulfilling anymore. Not because of the kids, but unfortunately because of the parents and the administration. To make a long story short, I moved on to working for a marketing company and then six months later got the opportunity to begin my career in the insurance industry. I started out selling health insurance in February of 2006, and I've since moved on to become a broker and work with a couple of different firms where I'm able to help people. My passion is to help people protect themselves and their families from any kind of potential catastrophe. And that's what helps me to stay in this industry. Because ever since I first started in the industry, I've learned a lot, and I'm still learning a lot. But at the same time, I have also seen a lot of things that shouldn't have happened to people because of unscrupulous agents that only cared about themselves and wanted to make as much money as they could. Unfortunately, that's the reality of the industry; there are a few bad apples out there like any other industry. And that's what makes it hard on honest people like myself that work with high integrity and high character in the best interests of the client. This is what keeps me moving and keeps me in the industry, helping people, making sure they and their family will be ok, and will be fully protected. And not get scammed.

"What is the purpose of insurance anyway? Why do I need it? I don't need it. Nothing's ever going to happen." I've heard this many times over the course of my career and the reason is to protect against the "what if's". What if something happens? For instance, I've heard, "I'm never going to get in a car accident". Well, never say never. What if you get in that car accident and you don't have your auto insurance? You won't be able to fix your car and might be held liable (especially if you're at fault) if people get hurt. Not only your passengers, but also the passengers in the other car too. The main thing with any type of insurance is that it is all about protecting yourself, your assets, and - most importantly - your family. Because if you don't have it you're opening yourself up for a lot of liability, and then you have to come up with all that money to cover whatever has happened. But more about that later.

What I want you to take away from this chapter is that the purpose of insurance is to help protect you and your family from any kind of catastrophe or accident so you and your family will not experience financial hardship.

Notes

Notes

Chapter 2
Auto Insurance
"Driving to protect my family"

From Wikipedia: "Vehicle insurance (also known as gap insurance, car insurance, or motor insurance) is insurance purchased for cars, trucks, motorcycles and other road vehicles." The purpose of auto insurance is to protect yourself financially from bills as a result of any kind of physical damage to your vehicle or bodily injury resulting from a collision and any kind of liability that could happen as a result of an accident, which should really be called a collision.; because technically there is no such thing as an accident. There are seven primary areas of auto insurance coverage: Bodily Injury Liability, Property Damage, Medical Payments, Collision, Comprehensive, Under/Uninsured, and elective coverages.

In most states, auto insurance is mandatory. If you don't have it then you could have your license suspended or revoked. The amount of minimum coverage you are required to have varies from state to state because the laws and regulations vary from state to state. For instance, in Illinois you have to have at least $20,000/$40,000 worth of Bodily Injury Liability coverage. What does that mean? Basically a $20,000/$40,000 policy means that it includes $20,000 worth of coverage for each person in the other vehicle and a maximum of $40,000 worth of coverage for the whole accident. If you have a $250,000/$500,000 policy you have $250,000 worth of coverage for each person and a maximum of $500,000 worth of coverage for the whole accident. Don't forget, this covers only the passengers in the other vehicle if you are at fault. If you're not at fault that's when the other company may potentially have to pay. Suppose you have a $250,000/$500,000 policy and you're in a collision. Two people in the other car are hurt. Let's say one person has $100,000 worth of medical bills and the other one has medical bills of $200,000. That's a total of $300,000. You're all set; you don't have to worry about it. Everything is covered. But what do you do in the event that their medical bills are even higher? That's where an umbrella policy, or a personal liability policy, would come into play if you have it. Typically people get a $1 million umbrella that would provide coverage above and beyond that $250,000/$500,000 limit of your auto insurance policy.

Property damage is the coverage to fix the damage to the other vehicle. Typically the amount available is between $100,000 and $400,000. An insurance company figures out how much it will cost to fix the vehicle by having an insurance adjuster inspect it to determine how much damage there is. Your insurance company pays the cost of repairs up to the limit listed on your policy. If the cost of the repairs exceeds this amount, you are personally responsible for paying the difference. A $100,000 policy might not cover all of the repairs on a Ferrari or Tesla, for example.

Medical payments coverage is used to cover the cost of medical care for your passengers. The highest coverage available is usually $10,000 per person, but there are some companies that offer a limit as high as $25,000. If you have a $1,000 limit that means that your insurance company will only cover $1,000 worth of medical treatment for your passenger. Often people say "That's what health insurance is for." Here's the problem with that. If your health insurance has a $5,000 deductible, that's $4,000 out of pocket for your passenger. So that's why, in my opinion, you should have at least $5,000 to $10,000 in medical payments coverage.

Collision coverage is the coverage to fix the damage to your vehicle. This is where your deductible comes into play. Here again the insurance company will figure out how much it will cost to fix the vehicle by having an insurance adjuster inspect it to determine how much damage there is. Then you pay your deductible (anywhere from $50 up to $2,500) and the insurance company covers the rest of the cost of repair. But only up to the Kelly Blue Book value. The Kelly Blue Book is an auto industry standard value listing of every vehicle ever manufactured. If the cost of repairs is equal to or more than the Blue Book value it will be totaled. The insurance company will then write you a check for the value of your vehicle less your deductible and the vehicle will be sent to the junkyard. You then get to shop for another vehicle!

Comprehensive coverage is similar to collision because it covers your vehicle. It works just like collision, but as its name implies, it covers your vehicle when something happens to it other than hitting something. This can range from being broken into to catching on fire, or even being in a flood. Your deductible still applies, as do Blue Book value limits.

Under/Uninsured coverage protects you in the event that you are involved in a collision with someone who either doesn't have any insurance at all or doesn't have enough insurance in their policy to cover the cost of your medical bills or repairs to your vehicle. Suppose you are involved in a collision with an uninsured motorist. Because they do not have insurance and you do, they are automatically at fault, even if you caused the collision. When they are 100% liable your insurance company will go after them to pay all the bills. That's the upside. The downside is if your car needs to be fixed right away (assuming that you have full coverage - more about that coming up) then you will have to pay your deductible. If you have a $500 deductible, you pay the first $500 and then the insurance company pays the rest of that bill up to the Blue Book value, just as it does with Collision coverage. When they get their money back from that uninsured motorist you will be reimbursed the amount of your deductible. If the other driver in a collision is found at fault but does not have enough insurance to cover the cost of your medical bills or repairs to your vehicle this coverage on your policy would also kick in. Once again you would pay your deductible and your insurance company would cover your medical bills and vehicle repairs up to the limits in your Bodily Injury Liability coverage and Property Damage coverage or Blue Book value, whichever is lower. If your insurance company gets their money back from the underinsured driver you may be reimbursed the amount of your deductible.

Elective coverages include Rental Coverage and Roadside Assistance add ons. Rental Coverage helps pay for a rental car when your vehicle is being repaired as the result of a collision. Limits apply here too. If your coverage is $50/$500 that means the insurance company will pay up to $50 a day, and up to a total of $500 toward the cost of a rental car. You can also add on Roadside Assistance or Towing coverage. This works similar to a motor club such as AAA, but may be less expensive. If you break down and you need to get your vehicle towed to a shop you would call an 800 number and they send a tow truck to pick you up and tow your vehicle to a repair shop. Be aware that even if it's not as the result of a collision this tow could be counted as a claim against you, depending on the fine print of your policy. I'd rather pay a little bit more and use AAA and not have to worry about my auto insurance going up because I had to get a tow or I locked my keys in the car.

Now let's talk a little bit about how insurance companies determine who is at fault, or liable, in a collision. Most people would think that the person who gets the ticket is 100% liable and their insurance company should be responsible for covering all of the losses as a result of the collision. This is true if you live in an "at fault" state. These states have passed laws declaring just that, if you are found at fault for an accident your insurance is required to cover 100% of the losses. In the rest of the states the insurance companies assess the blame. They ask what percentage of the damage did you cause and what percentage of the damage did the other party cause. Very rarely will they say a collision is 100% someone's fault. Let's say that you got rear ended. The other party's insurance company may feel that if you weren't there it would have never happened, therefore you are 2% at fault and your insurance company is responsible for 2% of the losses. Consider this scenario: you went through a yellow light and someone hit you. Technically, they were in the wrong, not you. And more often than not, law enforcement would issue them a ticket. In an at-fault state their insurance company would cover all losses 100%. In all other states the insurance company will assess the blame. If you had already entered the intersection and then the light turned yellow, the other insurance company may say "Now wait a minute, you shouldn't have been in that intersection because it was a yellow light and you went through it." Should you have stopped? No, of course you should keep going, because it's safer to keep going. However, they're going to try to assess some of that blame on you. They may say "Yes, our driver was at fault, but you should have anticipated the yellow light and been more cautious. We will take 80% of the blame and pay 80% of the costs." And then the insurance companies basically fight it out and decide who's going to pay what in a process called subrogation.

Do you live in an at-fault state? Check out the list at unvarnishedtruthbook.com to find out.

Have you ever wondered how your insurance company determines what your premium will be? There are some factors that you can't control and a few that you can. Things such as:

- Gender - Typically, males will pay more than females.
- Age - The younger you are, the higher your premiums will be.
- Driving Record - Insurance companies also look at your Motor Vehicle Record (MVR), more commonly known as your driving record. Moving violations, such as speeding or running red lights, things of that nature, will count as points against you. The more points you have, the higher your premium will be. The more collisions you have, the higher your premium will be, unless those are not-at-fault accidents. An example would be if you got rear ended, or your car was parked and someone hit it. These are considered not-at-fault accidents. Whether or not you've ever been convicted of driving under the influence would also be reported on your MVR and taken into consideration when calculating your premium amount.
- Marital Status - Statistics show that married drivers average fewer accidents, so they typically have lower premiums than single people.
- Vehicle Type - This includes things like style (sedan, little economy car, SUV, etc.), whether it's a car that's stolen a lot, and what color it is.
- Distance Driven - If you only drive 7,000 miles a year you're going to pay a lot less than if you're driving 10,000 or 20,000 miles a year. Now, they don't expect you to be spot on exact I'm going to drive 9,950 miles a year. As an example, if you say "I only drive, 10,000 miles a year" and you drive 10,100 miles next year, they're not going to make a big deal about that. However, if you say "I'm going to drive 10,000 miles this year" and you actually drive 20,000 miles that would be a problem. It is important that you are honest in what you report to your insurance company about the distance you drive. It doesn't matter if you under or over report, either

way it can affect whether or not your insurance company pays a claim.

- Vehicle Use - Do you just drive it for pleasure and getting to and from work or do you drive it for work too?
- Credit Rating - The higher your credit score, the lower your premium; the lower your credit score, the higher your premium. Why is that? Insurance companies believe this is a predictor of your risk. Typically drivers with good credit scores are more financially stable, more responsible, and they have the means to maintain their vehicles. At least that's what the insurance companies believe.
- Home Ownership - Again the insurance companies believe you are financially more responsible than a renter, so if you own a home or condo you may qualify for a discount. There is another way this can contribute to a lower premium, though. If you get a homeowners policy and an umbrella policy from the same company as your auto insurance policy your premium may be lower through what's called bundling, or a multi policy discount.

A question I'm often asked is "How can I lower the premiums on my auto insurance?" One way is to have higher deductibles. I've seen policies with $2,500 deductibles. The problem with a deductible this high is that you have to pay the first $2,500 of a repair out of your own funds. It's not like homeowners insurance (which I go into detail about in the next chapter) where they'll just deduct this amount from the check they cut. This is because with auto insurance the company usually pays the repair shop directly. That's why you want to have an amount that's manageable for you. Keep in mind the lower the deductible, the higher your premium will be. Another way is to have lower liability amounts. Keep in mind that the higher your liability amounts are, the more protected you are; I would be very cautious about lowering these amounts.

Another way you can lower your premiums is to have liability only coverage. This is not an option for you if you have a leased vehicle or if you have taken out a loan that uses your vehicle as collateral. In both of those instances the law says that you must maintain full coverage insurance, meaning you have to carry Bodily Injury Liability coverage, Property Damage coverage, Medical Payments coverage, Collision coverage, and Comprehensive coverage. But if you own your vehicle free and clear and are willing to take the risk you can get what is called Liability Only Coverage. This type of policy only covers the cost of the other car in the event that you are found at fault. Your car is not covered and you will have to pay out of your own funds to get your vehicle fixed. People typically get liability only coverage when they have older cars. For example, if a car is 20 years old and it has 100,000 miles or more people typically will say "I don't want to spend that much money on premiums. If I get into a car accident they're not going to cover me that much anyway because there's not much value left in my car. They would probably just total it, so no big deal". Yes, you will have lower premiums, but remember that if you are at fault Liability Only coverage will not pay to fix any property damage to your car.

One final note about reducing premium costs. There are new products, technologies, and gimmicks emerging every day. Some good, some bad, and some that seem good on the surface but turn out to be bad. One such item started with Progressive in 1998. It was a GPS-based device in your car that tracked your driving behavior and reported the results to the company so they knew when you were speeding, when you were not speeding, how many miles you actually drove, and things like that. When customers complained about the cost of the device the pilot program was ended in 2000. Since then many companies have introduced black box technology. As in the black box in an airplane that records everything. Similar technology is used in cars to report many metrics to your insurance company. That can lower your premium by a large amount. However, if they see that you're speeding a lot (because now they can determine if you're going 50 miles an hour in a 20 mile an hour zone consistently) or that you are driving in a reckless manner your premiums can go up. You have to think very carefully about whether or not you really want to have all that information available to your insurance company. Any time you are offered a new way to lower your premiums be sure to look at it from all sides before you make a final decision.

Next I'll show you how to protect your home.

But first, go to unvarnishedtruthbook.com for your free checklist on what to do when you are in involved in an auto collision.

Notes

Notes

Chapter 3
Home Owner's Insurance
"Safely Sleeping In My Home"

The actual first home owner's policy was introduced in September of 1950 and it was designed to cover fire losses, theft, and personal property. Today Wikipedia defines Home Owner's Insurance as "Home insurance, also commonly called hazard insurance or home owner's insurance (often abbreviated in the US real estate industry as HOI), is a type of property insurance that covers a private residence." What that means in laymen's terms is that it covers your home. There are a lot of things that you have to consider when you buy your home owner's insurance policy. The first is what type of dwelling you have because there's a big difference between coverage for a house, coverage for a condo, and coverage for an apartment. We'll get into in the details of condo and apartment policies a little bit later.

When the policy covers a house there are multiple parts to it. Coverage A is for the dwelling. It covers exactly what it says it does – your house. Coverage B is for any other structures, such as a detached garage or shed. Coverage C is for your personal property. Coverage D is for loss of use or additional living benefits. In the event of a total loss (due to fire or natural disaster, for example) if you are required to make other living arrangements such as staying in a hotel or renting an apartment, this part would cover those costs. Liability coverage is in case any guest gets hurt or their personal belongings are damaged. And finally there is medical coverage. Again this covers exactly what it says it does – the medical bills incurred when a guest is hurt. The higher the liability limit the greater the protection that you will have for yourself. A liability limit of $500,000 would mean that you are protected for up to $500,000. Notice how there are limits to this. In the event that someone slips and falls going down your front stairs, you are liable for that. That's why it's called liability insurance. And this is where a lot of people say "I've got $500,000 in liability coverage; I don't need that much in medical." Keep in mind that medical insurance typically covers the cost of the deductible of the injured person's health insurance, not the entire cost of their treatment. I always advise my clients to have no less than $5,000, but the higher the medical the better.

Sewer back up is an optional coverage that many people assume is covered under the dwelling coverage. It is not automatically included; you have to make sure that it is specifically listed. This coverage takes care of any water damage caused by plumbing issues. This can be anything from backed up drains to burst pipes or overflowing bathtubs, just to name a few. You should have at least $5,000 in coverage for sewer back up.

Deductibles for Home Owner's Insurance can be anywhere from $0 to $10,000, but a typical deductible is $1,000 - $2,500. It depends on how much risk you want to have and how much you want to pay. The higher the deductible the lower your premium, because you're taking on more of the risk. If you want lower premiums and have money set aside just in case and say "Go ahead and give me a $5,000 deductible." that could save you money on your premiums. As with Auto Insurance you pay the amount of the deductible and the insurance company pays the rest of the cost. Let's take a hail damaged roof for example. Your insurance company inspects the roof and estimates that it will cost $10,000 to fix. If your deductible is $5,000 they're only going to cut you a check for $5,000 and you have to come up with the other $5,000 to pay for that roof.

Let's talk about how you can lower your premiums on your Home Owner's Insurance. Much like Auto Insurance there are some things that will earn you discounts. Some you can control and some you can't. Things like:

- Distance to fire station - if you live close to a fire station you will get discounts. This is because if there's a fire at your house, the fire department's going to get there a lot quicker if you're living less than a mile from the fire station than if you're five miles away. That means it's more likely that there's going to be a lot more damage, which means a lot more exposure to the insurance company.
- Sprinklers – Having these guarantees a discount. They put the fire out faster, sometimes even before the fire department arrives. This reduces the amount of damage the insurance company has to cover, and they pass the savings along to you.
- Smoke Detectors – These too will lower your premium because the people in the house are alerted to a fire faster and can call for help quicker as well as get out and prevent bodily injury.
  Be aware with both sprinklers and fire alarms it is important that you are honest in what you report to your insurance company. If there's a fire and you've told them that you have sprinklers and/or smoke detectors but they see that you really didn't that could be considered fraud. They could then deny your claim because you lied to them.
- Multiple Policies - As we discussed in the previous chapter, if you go with the same carrier for your auto insurance you'll get a discount as well.

- Security Measures - A security monitoring system such as ADT will also qualify you for a discount. Insurer approved locks such as a bolt lock may qualify you for a discount, too.

Another important thing that I wish everyone would do at least once a year is document your belongings. The easiest way to do this is by video taping every room in your house. Ideally this should be done twice a year, but at the very least once every 12 months. Zoom in on your TV to show the make and model. It would be great if you can include the serial number, too. Don't forget to document your laptop, tablet, cell phone, high end kitchen appliances, gaming equipment, jewelry, musical instruments, and any other high value items you own. It's important to include every room in the house, especially if you have high end or custom finishes on your walls, cabinets, counter tops, etc. Painting, wall hangings and other décor and furniture should also be featured in your home video. Without this there is no way to prove exactly what you had in the event of theft or fire. Especially fire if the receipts and users guides are destroyed.

Speaking of everything being destroyed in a fire, that reminds me of a point that most of my clients have never heard of until they met me. It's called laws and ordinance. If your city passes a law that requires changes to your existing structure such as sprinklers you may not be required to add them to your existing home. This is called being grandfathered in. But, if you build a new house they would be required. In the event of a fire that causes a total loss, when you rebuild you will have to add those sprinklers to your home. In most policies there is only a provision for 10% coverage for things that are added in because of laws & ordinance. If that sprinkler system adds $100,000 to the cost of your rebuild and your policy only provides 10% coverage your insurance company will only cover $10,000 of the cost. You will have to find a way to pay the other $90,000. You can increase the laws & ordinance coverage to 100% if you are willing to pay the price for it. I recommend that my clients increase it gradually over time so they aren't hit with sticker shock in the first year. I definitely recommend that they have at least 50% though.

Condo Insurance is slightly different from Home Owner's. There aren't multiple parts because it only covers from the studs in. This means not only the stuff inside, the contents or your personal property, but also the walls, the floors, and the ceilings. Common areas, such as hallways outside of your unit and the exterior of the building would be covered under the association's policy, not yours. As with Home Owner's Insurance, though you pick how much liability coverage you want to have. The higher the better, because you never know what may happen. If your bathtub overflows into the unit below you and ruins their Persian rug, you are liable for the damages.

You have to watch out for the laws & ordinances coverage in a condo policy too. It works the same way here as it does in Home Owner's Insurance. Review the paragraph on it above if you skimmed over it thinking it didn't apply. It does.

Renter's Insurance is even simpler. Because as a renter you don't have to worry about what to do if the whole apartment building burns down, all you have to worry about is your belongings and your liability if someone gets hurt in your apartment.

Turn the page to learn how to navigate the ACA.

Notes

Notes

Chapter 4
Health Insurance
"Prolonging My Dash"

Wikipedia states that "in the United States health insurance is any program that helps pay for medical expenses whether through privately purchased insurance, social insurance, or a social welfare program funded by the government." Most people get their health insurance one of two ways. The first way is to buy it yourself. At one point in time all health insurance policies were private or individual policies and you had to medically qualify. This meant you would go through a process called underwriting. This entailed answering a series of health questions. If you suffered from certain illnesses or conditions the insurance company had two choices. They could either decline all coverage for you or they could exclude that one illness or condition. As an example, if an applicant was diagnosed with diabetes the insurance company would either decline to insure them or go ahead and insure them but exclude anything related to diabetes. That changed in 2010 when the Affordable Care Act was passed. It was designed to extend healthcare coverage to people who did not have it for any number of reasons. Maybe they didn't medically qualify, maybe they couldn't afford it. The Affordable Care Act is known by several different names. It is commonly referred to as Obama Care but it is also sometimes referred to as ACA plans. A lot of people think "The premiums are expensive. How is this affordable?" The affordable part comes with what's called a subsidy. Whether or not you get a subsidy and how much that subsidy would be depends upon your income level . Your income level is figured out by how much taxable income you have. And if you say "I'm still not going to get health insurance because I don't need it, I'm never going to use it and I'm not going to waste that money," you will be penalized.

Where does one start when they've decided to sign up for coverage? In order to sign up go to www.healthcare.gov and pick your plan. Some of the things to be aware of with these plans are:

- You have a deductible. As with all of the other coverages we've discussed so far, a deductible is the set amount that you pay up front. If you have a $6,000 deductible, you pay the first $6,000 of your healthcare costs.
- Your coverage after the deductible is paid (sometimes referred to as being met, as in "He met his deductible last month, so he doesn't have to pay anything for the rest of the year.") varies depending on the plan you've chosen and is called co-insurance. If you have a 100% plan and are hospitalized with a $6,000 deductible, you have to pay the first $6,000 and after that everything is covered.

If you have an 80/20 plan, after the deductible the insurance company pays 80% and you pay the other 20% of the rest of the costs. Let's go back to that example of a $6,000 deductible with an 80/20 plan. You pay the first $6,000 plus 20% of the costs above and beyond the $6,000. This is where people think, "Holy cow this is going to cost me a lot of money." Potentially, yes. However, on plans that cover less than 100% there is something called maximum out of pocket. This sets a maximum amount that you are required to pay. If your maximum out of pocket is $10,000 you'd pay the $6,000 deductible and then no more than $4,000 of the remaining costs.

I said there are two ways that most people get health insurance. The second is through Group Plans. Group health insurance means that you are fortunate enough to have a job that offers benefits. Typically to qualify for group health insurance you have to be a full time employee. This is defined as an hourly employee working 40 or more hours a week. Salaried employees are automatically included in the group.

How does group health insurance work now that the Affordable Care Act has been passed? First, there is no pre-existing condition provision. If you have no pre-existing conditions you're healthy; you never have to use the health insurance. That's great! But if you have a heart problem, cancer, diabetes or any other ongoing disease that is called a pre-existing condition. Now the insurance companies have to automatically offer you coverage as well as cover anything that happens as a result of those pre-existing conditions. That's what makes Group Health Plans a very good option. I always tell people, more so with the people that have Medicare (more about Medicare coverage later in this chapter), that if you are on a group plan, especially after you're retired, a lot of times that group health plan is better than getting a Medicare supplement and getting your Part D because you would have what Medicare calls "credible coverage". Stay where you're at because more often than not you have great coverage.

There are typically two types of group plans, Health Maintenance Organizations (HMOs) and Preferred Provider Organizations (PPOs). With an HMO, the HMO is made up of a network of doctors, and you can only go to the doctors in that network. You must choose a Primary Care Physician (PCP) when you enroll and if you want or need to bee seen by a specialist you have see your PCP to get a referral for the specialist. Usually you only have to pay a co-pay for any covered services and the insurance company pays for all charges above that amount, though the co-pay amount my vary from service to service. For instance, you might pay a $30 co-pay to see your PCP, but $50 for an appointment with a specialist and $100 for an Emergency Room visit. Choosing an HMO allows for predictable out-of-pocket expenses thanks to the co-pay model of payment.

With a PPO there is also a network of doctors, but you can go to doctors outside of that network too. Just keep in mind if you go out of the network your costs will be higher. PPOs generally follow the deductible/co-insurance model of payment. This means you have less predictable expenses. Once again maximum out-of-pockets are set so you know in advance the maximum you will have to pay in a certain period of time (usually a year). The deductible portion may be $500, but it could be as high as $1,000 - $2,500, or even $5,000. Because this is a group plan, the employer chooses the specifics of the plan, including deductible amount and it is the same for everyone who participates in that plan. What the employer wants to offer or even can afford comes into play here because typically lower deductibles raise the premiums for group health insurance, especially since the ACA was passed.

Keep in mind if you are fortunate enough to have the group health insurance that means that you have a full time job. Congratulations. For the people that are part time, obviously you would not qualify for group plans and that's when you would have to go on one of the "Obama Care" plans.

If you decide you still can't afford and don't want an ACA plan there are other alternative plans that will allow you to avoid paying the penalty. They may be less expensive than health insurance from "Obamacare" or a group plan.

For more information on these plans visit
unvarnishedtruthbook.com.

There are two other ways to obtain ACA compliant healthcare insurance coverage, but you have to qualify for them.

Medicare is the Federal health insurance program for people over 65 as well as people under 65 that qualify for coverage due to having a disability. The under 65 qualifiers are put on Social Security Disability Insurance (SSDI). People diagnosed with "end stage renal disease" may qualify for Medicare as well.

Medicare coverage is comprised of Part A, which covers inpatient hospital stays and skilled nursing care, Part B which covers doctor's visits and any kind of testing or procedures done on an outpatient basis, next up you can choose a way to reduce your costs with either Part C, an HMO equivalent option, or a supplement plan (read on to learn more about these), and finally the coverage is rounded out with Part D to cover prescription medications.

With Medicare a lot of people think that they're entitled to insurance coverage at no cost because they have been paying into it through Federal Insurance Contributions Act (FICA). The determining factor of whether or not Medicare Part A coverage can be obtained "for free" or no premium is that you have to have worked at least 40 quarters over the course of your working career in order to receive your Part A with no premium. This is equivalent to 10 years, (4 quarters per year x 10 years = 40 quarters).

Right now the premium for Part B is based on your income. The more money you make the higher your premium will be. As of 2015 the lowest premium is $104.90 a month. This premium will be taken directly out of your social security check.

If you are not drawing social security you will have to make arrangements to pay your premiums.

If your Medicare card has a letter "A" that means that you put in your 40 quarters. A letter "T" means that you are still working and you are not yet drawing social security. And a letter "D" means dependent. This is when you have not worked the 40 quarters but your spouse has and now you are on "their" Medicare.

Medicare uses the term "assignment" for the amount that a provider will receive as payment. This is because a provider bills their usual and customary fee and Medicare negotiates it down. When they agree on an amount, the provider is said to accept the fee assigned by Medicare. The provider has the option of billing you for up to 15% of the difference between the usual and customary fee and the assignment, called the "gap." Both Part A and Part B have deductibles and then 80/20 coverage kicks in. Medicare only pays 80% of the assignment which means if you have absolutely no other coverage in place you have to come up with that other 20% plus the deductibles and the gap. Historically the deductibles have been going up every year, so that could be a huge problem for people. You've already worked hard enough all these years and now in your retirement years; you can't afford to have that that kind of gap. There are two options for additional coverage.

First, you can get a Medicare Supplement plan or Medigap policy. There are different plans/policies available, each named with a different letter of the alphabet from A through N and providing slightly different coverage. Many companies offer Medicare Supplement plans, also known as Med Sups. Each company is governed by the Office of Centers for Medicare/Medicaid Services (CMS) which ensures they all offer the exact same benefits in each plan. The only difference from one provider or insurance company to the other is the premium they charge. Some people feel that Med Sups can be expensive, with costs for premiums ranging from $100 to $400 a month depending on where you live, your age, your gender, smoking habits, and what company you choose to purchase a plan from. As an example of how a Med Sup can help cover costs, let's consider Plan F. Plan F will pay the other 20% of the assignment as well as the gap that Medicare did not pay for. Notice how I say "pay for" not "cover" because if Medicare does not cover a procedure the Medicare Supplement will not cover it either in most cases. For example, acupuncture is not covered by Medicare; therefore your Medicare Supplement will not cover acupuncture.

The second option for additional coverage is a program called Part C or Medicare Advantage. This is a good alternative for people who cannot afford a Medicare supplement. The premium for Medicare Advantage coverage is typically $0. That is typically for an HMO network of providers. This HMO network works very similar to the HMO in a group plan. You have to go a doctor within that network and there are co-pays for doctor's visits, procedures done, co-pays for in-patient hospital stays, as well as co-insurance for procedures. Remember that there is a difference between co-pays and co-insurance; just as with group health insurance, a co-pay is a flat rate and co-insurance is a percentage. Typically Medicare Advantage plans have a maximum out-of-pocket, even on the co-pays. Keep in mind though that even if you have Medicare Advantage coverage you will have to continue to pay your Part B premium. It will continue to come out of your social security check.

And finally, Part D covers the cost of your prescription medication. If you have a Medicare supplement you have to pay a premium every month for this coverage and there may also be deductibles as well as co-pays. Similar to the Med Sup plans, Part D works the same way no matter which insurance company you go with. They all have the coverage gap, more commonly referred to as the "donut hole". They all have the initial coverage stage, the coverage gap (donut hole), and the catastrophic stage. The big difference is how much the premium is and what the co-pays are as well. If Part D coverage is included or embedded with Medicare Advantage coverage the premium is typically $0.

The last type of health insurance we are going to discuss in this book is Medicaid. Medicaid is the state insurance program for people with lower incomes, administered and regulated by each particular state, and paid for through state taxes, essentially. Each state has its own regulations pertaining to how much you can make a year as well as what kind of or how much coverage you would have. Maybe someone cannot afford health insurance when they try to get an ACA plan. That's when they would be placed on Medicaid. There are basically two types of Medicaid programs. In the "full" Medicaid program everything is covered. All you do is you go to a doctor that has been approved and agreed to accept Medicaid, and then the state pays the provider (the doctor or hospital) directly. If you have what's called a spend down, that is how much you would have to pay every month for your healthcare. Even though it is not a deductible, it may help to understand it if you think of this like a deductible. For instance if you have a $500 spend down that means you would have to pay the first $500 of medical expenses either when you go to a doctor, or God forbid, you have to have some kind of surgical procedure, and then Medicaid pays the rest.

If your income goes up and you're earning more money than the maximum allowed threshold you can lose your Medicaid coverage. And this may be a reason that a lot of people don't work; maybe they can't work or maybe they don't want to work because they don't want to lose their Medicaid.

One final thought about health insurance. You can also go out and get what's called an indemnity plan. A big problem with this option is that it is not an ACA compliant plan and you will still have to pay the penalty. You may say "Yeah, but the premiums are a lot cheaper over here, so between that and the penalty I'm still coming out ahead." Another problem with an indemnity plan, or an indemnity-style plan, is that it pays a certain amount of dollars for a procedure. For example, if you go in for a surgery, and your indemnity plan pays $50,000 for this particular procedure and the bill comes back at $100,000 you're on the hook for the other $50,000 because the indemnity plan covers a flat rate. That being said basically what happens is the insurance company will always come in and try to negotiate with the hospital to drive the price down. And that's where the games are always being played between the doctors/ hospitals and the insurance companies. The healthcare providers are pointing the fingers at the insurance company and saying well they're not paying enough and the insurance companies are saying the healthcare providers are charging too much. Who pays in the end? You, the consumer.

I hope that you learned something new about protecting and prolonging your dash - in other words, your life right now. Keep reading because the best is yet to come. In the very next chapter I will show you how to protect your income.

Don't forget to visit unvarnishedtruthbook.com to sign up for my free newsletter.

Notes

Notes

Chapter 5
Disability Insurance
"Protecting Your Paycheck"

Wikipedia defines Disability Insurance, often called DI or Disability Income Insurance or Income Protection as "a form of insurance that insures the beneficiaries' earned income against the risk that a disability creates a barrier for a worker to complete the core functions of their work." What that means is in the event that you get hurt, whether it is on the job or off the job, your income is protected because disability insurance is a private insurance policy; it's not through your job, that's workers comp, which we will talk about in the next chapter. This is a way for self-employed people to protect themselves because they may not have workers comp due to the fact that they're a one man shop. Some good examples are a doctor or a lawyer. If a doctor gets hurt and he cannot perform his duties as a doctor the disability income protection will provide money. Typically people buy disability insurance to protect their income up to a certain percentage; anywhere from 50-60%. The idea behind it is that you won't be on it forever. It discourages people from deciding they don't want to work and pretending they are hurt; that's called fraud. You can't fake an injury or you can't prolong it because the insurance company may come and check up on you. A lot of times there are limits to it such as a short term policy where it's only for just that - a short amount of time; anywhere from 6 months to a year. Sometimes you have a long term disability insurance policy which could be anywhere from 2 to 5 years.

You can get your own individual disability insurance even if you are an employee. It would work alongside your worker's comp if you got injured on the job. If you have a disability insurance policy you can use the income protection plan and draw an income anywhere from 50-60% depending upon the state that you live in.

There is an elimination period. This is a set amount of time that it will not cover you; think of it like a deductible. For instance, if you have a 60 day elimination period that means for the first 60 days that you are disabled it will not pay out. You have to wait 60 days for it to start. Typically the elimination period is 0 days, 30 days, or 90 days.

There's also what's called Business Overhead Expense disability insurance, or BOE. This is for self-employed people in the event they become disabled and they cannot work anymore for whatever reason. This coverage will reimburse the business for all the overhead expenses; such as the rent, mortgage, utilities, if they have a lease or any other kind of accounting, billing, business insurance premiums, and will also cover the employees' salaries. Property taxes and any kind of monthly expenses are also covered under this business overhead policy. It's a great option to have when you are a business owner. You definitely want to protect your business because if you don't have this in place and you become disabled and can't work anymore, the money stops coming in which could hurt or even kill your business. I can't stress enough how important this coverage is if you are self-employed. You want to protect not only your paycheck but you want to protect your business as well.

Read on to learn how to protect yourself on the job.

Notes

Chapter 6
Worker's Comp
"Your Bill or Mine?"

Wikipedia defines Worker's Comp or Worker's Compensation as "a form of insurance providing wage replacement and medical benefits to employees injured in the course of employment in exchange for mandatory relinquishment of the employee's right to sue his or her employer for the torte of negligence." Wow, there's a mouthful for you. Essentially what this means is that in the event that you are hurt on the job - notice how I said **on the job** - you will be covered and your income will continue. That being said, you will not get your full wages. The amount of what you will receive is typically between 50-65% of your regular paycheck. The reason why you don't get 100% of your wages is because they want you to go back to work as soon as you can. It's not meant to be compensation for the rest of your life.

In addition to receiving a portion of your wages all of the medical costs of treating your injuries are covered as well. This is an area where fraud could potentially happen. Let's say you're at home fixing your gutters and you fall off the ladder on a Saturday. You may be tempted to come limping into work and think that nobody will ever know if you fake an injury at work. Obviously that is fraud. If or when they find out that you have made a fraudulent claim you can be fined heavily, go to jail or both.

However, you should always report it if you ever get hurt at work, no matter how minor it might seem; even if you think "Eh, it doesn't hurt me. No big deal." The same rules apply whether you're working in a factory or an office setting. If you get hurt, no matter how minor it is, always report it. Because if you don't report it and two days later you start feeling sore or your symptoms get worse, you may not be covered. As an example, you're an office worker and you trip and fall in the office, or bump your head while reaching for something under the desk. And you say ow and rub your head a bit, but don't think much of it. Then a couple days later you start getting dizzy spells because of that bumped head. Or your leg is hurting because of the trip and fall. Because you did not report either accident, technically your employer is not liable. Not reporting is just as serious as committing fraud by claiming an accident happened at work when it really happened at home.

Another thing that workers compensation coverage takes into consideration is if there was negligence. In other words did you do something that you shouldn't have been doing to begin with? As an example, if you're working in a factory and you're supposed to be wearing protective eyewear, but you're not. And you get hurt because you weren't wearing the required eye protection. That's negligence on your part and your employer doesn't necessarily have to give you full workers comp. coverage. Usually the medical bills will get paid but you may not have a percentage of your wages provided. You must follow whatever safety procedures are required no matter what type of occupation you have or what kind of work environment you are in. Whether it's a factory or an office setting you always have to think safety. You don't want to put yourself, or anyone else for that matter, in harms way.

Next I'll show you how to stay home if you need long term care.

Business owners should visit unvarnishedtruthbook.com to learn how you can reduce your bottom line by saving on FICA taxes, compliments of the ACA.

Notes

Notes

Chapter 7
Long Term Care
"Take Me Home"

Wikipedia defines Long Term Care Insurance as "an insurance product sold in the United States, United Kingdom, and Canada that helps provide for the cost of long term care beyond a pre-determined period." What that means is if you cannot perform at least 2 out of 6 Activities of Daily Living (ADLs) (defined as a "trigger") you can now qualify to use Long Term Care insurance to cover the costs of either a nursing home or home health care. Now here's the thing, a lot of people, especially on Medicare think "Medicare will cover that." Yes, Medicare covers skilled nursing, as we talked about earlier. But they will not cover long term care. The big difference between skilled nursing is basically with skilled nursing you are getting better and you will not be there forever. Whereas with long term care you're either not getting better or you're getting worse and you're typically going to be there for a long time or possibly even until you die.

Long term care is not covered by Medicare or health insurance. Now, that being said, a lot of people say "Well, Medicaid pays for it." But before you even go on Medicaid there's what people call a "spend-down". What that means is you have to spend all of your assets down so that you are left with an amount that is under the threshold of allowable assets determined by each state. There's also a look back period. This is when the state looks over your finances for the last few years to see if you have transferred any assets to family members so that you aren't forced to spend them down. Depending on the state this period can be anywhere from 5 to 7 years. If you try to shelter your assets and it's within the look back period it is counted against you and they could force you to spend that down. Once you have spent your assets down then Medicaid steps in, you have to go into a Medicaid-approved facility, and if you're on Social Security you may no longer receive those benefits because Medicaid might take that automatically to pay for your long term care needs. That's why saying "I'll just go on Medicaid" is not a good thing to do. Spending all of your assets down means there may be nothing or next to nothing left to give as an inheritance to your children or grandchildren, whoever you want to give it to. Long Term Care insurance is how you would protect yourself, and more specifically your assets.

One way of getting Long Term Care coverage is to buy a Standalone Long Term Care insurance policy. With all Long Term Care coverage there is an elimination period. An elimination period means that if you have a need for long term care during the elimination period you will have to pay for that care, essentially you are not covered until the end of the elimination period. Make sure you know exactly what your elimination period is. For instance 90 days can be either 90 calendar days or 90 service days. Calendar days are just that, 90 days in a row. Ninety service days are completely different and may be a lot longer than 90 calendar days. If you have a nurse or caregiver coming in 3 days a week each of those days is a service day. After 90 calendar days you're nowhere close to 90 service days. Service days are usually seen in older policies. Policies written now typically specify calendar days. In order to use the benefits of the policy you have to show the insurance company that you cannot perform 2 or 3 of the 6 ADLs. Those are dressing, bathing, eating, toileting, transferring (getting in and out of bed), and walking. One of the potential problems with a standalone policy is that it's not indemnity style. What that means is that they don't write the check to you. Either they reimburse you after you show them the bill that you've paid, or you submit the bill to the insurance company and they will pay the facility directly. For example you require long term care and you may have a favorite aunt that is a nurse, or maybe even a retired nurse, and she wants to take care of you and get paid. If your insurance company pays on a reimbursement basis, she may not get paid because she's not "qualified". Even if she's acting as a caregiver, too bad. If your policy is an indemnity style policy, now you can go ahead and pay her to help you out because the insurance company will pay you without your having to show proof of a paid bill.

You might be wondering "What happens if I never use it"? You can add what is called a return of premium rider on there. This means that if you die and have never used it your beneficiary would get those premiums back. That being said, adding the rider does increase your premiums.

Another way to get this type of coverage is to get a long term care rider on your Life Insurance policy. The amount of Long Term Care coverage available this way is up to 2% of the death benefit, which would reduce the payment to your beneficiary when you die by the amount used on long term care. Typically this coverage is indemnity style. And as in the standalone you have to prove that you cannot perform 2 of the 6 ADLs.

A third way to get Long Term Care insurance is through an annuity. Many annuities have a long term care rider. And others are set up specifically for long term care. In an annuity if you never use that long term care your money is still going to accumulate and you don't have to worry about "wasting" all that money over the years for insurance that you never used. But if in fact you do have to use it, it's there for you. Think of it like putting it in two buckets. You've got the one bucket of cash that's accumulating cash; your money's making money for you, so it's in the accumulation phase. And the other bucket is your long term care benefit. You have a set amount and that's how much you're going to have. If you have $100,000 in the long term care bucket you can use it until you've spent $100,000 and that's it. There can be tax implications, so you have to make sure that it's structured the right way. Always talk to your tax professional; whether it be a CPA or an accountant.

Long term care is a great way for you to preserve your dignity. I hear a lot of people say "My kids will take care of me. My kids will take care of whatever I need." Have you had that conversation? Do you really want your children cleaning up after you; potentially changing your diapers? Do you really want to pass that burden down to them? And do your children want to take on that burden? That's the other thing that you have to consider as well. It is a very tough conversation to have, but that conversation needs to happen.

Next I'll show you how to protect your money.

Notes

Chapter 8
Annuities
"Time to protect my money"

An annuity is a financial contract in the form of an insurance product according to which a seller, or an issuer, typically a financial institution such as a life insurance company makes a series of future payments to a buyer, or an annuitant, in exchange for the immediate payment of a lump sum or a series of regular payments prior to the onset of the annuity. This is the definition that we see from Wikipedia. I'm sure you're asking "Alright Glen, what does all that mean?" Basically what it means is you put your money into this fund and it's a contract between you and an insurance company, typically a life insurance company, that says they will either pay you a lump sum after a certain amount of time or they will pay you installments over a period of time. When you are receiving the payments you are known as an annuitant. Now you are asking "Alright, what kinds of annuities are there and why should I get one?"

There are three popular types of annuities. The first one is a fixed annuity. A fixed annuity is just that, your interest rate is fixed at a certain percentage. This means that if you have a fixed annuity at 5% you will get a 5% interest rate no matter what happens to the stock market.

The next type is a variable annuity. This type of annuity is usually connected to bonds or mutual funds and the interest rate will fluctuate with the market. The upside to variable annuities is that they have a floor and that means a guarantee of a certain percent in interest. And you could make a large amount of money in interest. It all depends upon how the bond or the mutual funds perform. You get all the upside potential of the market without the downside risk.

The third type is a Fixed Indexed Annuity (FIA). This used to be called a fixed equity annuity. This annuity has a fixed percentage interest rate that is based on what the stock market does by being attached to an index. That index can be the S&P, the NASDAQ or maybe a global index. It is up to the insurance company to decide what index they are going to base it on. With this type of annuity, you only make money if the stock market goes up to a percentage that is capped. If the market stays the same or drops you make no interest. The way the caps works is when the stock market goes up you will earn interest up to the level of your cap. Let's say your cap is 15%. And the stock market goes up 20%. You would only earn 15% interest. I'm sure you're wondering who gets the other 5%. That would be the insurance company because they are taking all the risk. You may hear about something called a point to point basis in relation to a fixed index annuity. This refers to how the gains and losses are calculated. While the stock market fluctuates on a daily, hourly, or even minute by minute basis it would be vey cumbersome to calculate annuity interest that way. Some Fixed Index Annuities are reset on a monthly point to point while others are reset on a year to year point to point. It's important to look at your annuity contract to make sure that you understand exactly what you're getting yourself into.

There is a fourth type of annuity, but this one's not as common, so I didn't include it in my count. It's a Single Premium Immediate Annuity (SPIA). In this annuity you get to draw a monthly income from it right away, whereas with the other types of annuities you have to wait a certain amount of time before you can draw an income. Typically it could be anywhere from 7 to 10 years depending upon what the contract is. But here with the immediate annuity you draw the payments right away. Older people tend to like this option because they don't have to worry about outliving their income or their money because they will have that monthly income stream. This is where you really have to be careful with an immediate annuity, and it's something that a lot of people don't know: if it's not structured right you could potentially be taking a huge risk. If you start an immediate annuity and a year later you die, if it's not structured correctly the insurance company gets to keep the remainder of that money. This is why you have to make sure that there's something in the contract called period certain. So what that means is if you die within a certain period of time, then the rest of that money will be given to your beneficiary. This is where you and your trusted advisor /agent would work together to determine how long your certain period of time should be, or your "period certain". Usually this is between 10 and 20 years. Your beneficiary receives this money tax free and will have the choice of taking it as a monthly income stream, as a lump sum or they could roll it over into another type of investment. This is where your beneficiary needs to be careful because there could be tax implications. Any time you do anything with annuities or any other kind of financial vehicle like this, you should always consult a tax professional, whether it be a CPA or an accountant.

Annuities have their place but may not be the right thing for everyone. It all depends on what your goals are and how old you are. They are a great vehicle for people 50 or older. They may not be as good an option for someone in their 20s. I cannot stress enough that it may not be a good option for them because typically they may (again, strong emphasis on the may) be able to find a vehicle that will give them a higher return on their investment. At a younger age you can take a little bit more risk as opposed to nearing retirement age when you may not want to take as much risk. This is why you should be sure to sit down and talk with your advisor about your goals.

There are a few other less common annuities that may also be indicated in your situation. An impaired life annuity may be indicated in the case of a medical diagnosis which is severe enough to reduce the life expectancy of the annuitant. There is also a joint annuity, also called a survivor annuity. This is where the payments only stop upon the death of both of the annuitants. Your advisor should be able to tell you if either of these annuities would be best for your situation and goals.

Next I'll show you how to protect your family when you die.

Notes

Chapter 9
Life Insurance
"Life After My Dash"

Wikipedia defines life insurance as "A contract between an insured or an insurance policy holder and insurer where the insurer promises to pay a designated beneficiary a sum of money or the benefits in exchange for a premium upon the death of the insured person." It used to be that someone would buy a life insurance policy to protect not so much their life, but the life of the people that they were leaving behind. It's for your loved ones, your family; maybe you want to leave it to pay off all your debts. People buy life insurance for a lot of different reasons. Usually they buy life insurance to pay off debts and final expenses and to leave some money behind, perhaps to pay for college for the kids or grandkids. Or maybe they want to leave some money behind so their spouse can live on their income for the next 5-10 years. Before I got in the industry, I really didn't understand it. I always wondered "Why is it called life insurance? Because I don't benefit from it, someone else does and they don't get the benefit until I die. It should be called death insurance". And that's a legitimate argument for the life insurance of the 70s, 80s, even 90s. They are really death benefits. But now things have changed and the evolution of life insurance is amazing. That's right; Life Insurance has evolved over the years.

There are several types of life insurance policies you can get. The first is called term insurance. You hear a lot of "experts" out there telling you to buy term and invest the difference because you can get more insurance at a cheaper price. And that's very true. I do not dispute that one statement. But to give that advice as a blanket advice for everyone is not necessarily a good thing. Term has its place, no doubt about it. Term is very affordable and very "cheap". However, there are potential problems with it. Term insurance is purchased and is in force for a certain length of time, called a "term". This term can be anywhere from 10 – 30 years For instance, if you're 20 years old and you buy a 30 year term policy because you have a mortgage and want to make sure to leave money for your family to pay it off if you die. So you get $500,000 worth of coverage. At 20 years old that coverage in a term policy would be very cheap. But 30 years later you're 50 and you're still alive. What happens? Most term policies are guaranteed renewable. That means that it automatically renews once the term is up without proof of insurability. Basically that means you don't have to worry about whether you have an uninsurable disease like cancer or anything like that. They automatically renew it. Problem is you are now 30 years older and your premium will skyrocket. Perhaps you decide that you don't need that much coverage now because your mortgage has been paid off. That's great, but now the problem is that you've paid all that money over the past 30 years and you don't get it back. However, when you initially purchase the policy you can add a Return of Premium Rider. This means that after the 30 years are up you get all those premiums back tax free if you're still alive. However, it comes at a price. You do have to pay for that rider. And sometimes the rider can be expensive depending upon how old you are and what company you're working with.

What if you want to get life insurance where you don't have to worry about that? That would be whole life insurance. This is a permanent policy that accumulates cash value. The cash value accumulates over time at a level premium. This means you never have to worry about the premium going up. However, your cash value isn't really accumulating that fast and the interest rate isn't really all that good on a whole life policy They tend to be smaller policies called final expense policies. They are designed to have a smaller death benefit to cover all your final expenses including burial or cremation, probate, things like that. The death benefit could be anywhere from $5,000 up to $30,000 and is guaranteed. Essentially you pay forever and in the event that you die your beneficiaries will receive the death benefit tax free.

The third type is called Universal Life. With Universal Life there's greater flexibility in premium payments and it is a permanent policy. That means you never have to worry about the premiums going up. Your money earns interest in a Universal Life policy and you have the option of paying more than your monthly premium amount into the policy, or overfunding it so that your money can earn interest. In this way you are using your policy as a savings vehicle, similar to a savings account. One of the potential problems is that this type of policy is interest sensitive. When these policies first came out back in the '70s and '80s when the interest rates were great the average rate was 10-30% but then as the markets were going down and the stock market crashed, the interest rates went down at the same time. People had been underfunding their policies, depending on the high interest rate to earn money to cover their premiums and when the market crashed and interest rates dropped, the interest on the underfunded accounts no longer was enough to cover the premium. You also have to be careful that the cash value is always lower than the death benefit. It can never be more than the death benefit. That would fall into what's called an MEC or modified endowment contract and when that happens there's a lot of tax implications. So that's why you always have to watch out for that. If the insurance company sees that you're in danger of falling into an MEC they will send you a letter and give you the option of either raising the death benefit or decrease what you're putting into it.

Within the Universal Life family there's a policy known as an indexed universal life or an IUL. Much like the annuities that we talked about earlier, an IUL is connected to the performance of the market, specifically whatever index they tie it to. It could be a global index, the S&P or the stock market. There is a guarantee so you have the upside potential without the downside risk.

And then there is one other Universal Life policy called a Variable Universal Life, or a VUL. This one is similar to the variable annuities; the interest rate goes up and down, up and down, up and down and who knows what's going to happen next. There is no guarantee except for that death benefit as long as you continue to pay your premiums. You might wonder if the cash value can pay your premiums. Eventually yes, you can go ahead and say "You know money's tight. Please use the cash value for a couple months to pay the premiums." Keep in mind this does bring your cash value down. So you don't want to do that too often, especially in the early stages.

There's another life insurance policy called an Accidental Death policy. These are very inexpensive. The problem with them is that a lot of people think "I got a $500,000 life insurance policy for $10." Giving them a false sense of security. Just remember, you get what you pay for. If you die in an accident, that death benefit will be paid out. However, if you die as a result of a non-accident, perhaps a heart attack or cancer, or you commit suicide the life insurance company will not pay that out. I strongly advise my clients against getting an Accidental Death Insurance policy.

Remember how I said at the beginning of this chapter that life insurance has evolved? It used to be that you only got benefits when you die and someone else benefits from it. However times have changed and there are now some living benefits because you actually can benefit from it while you are living. With the universal and indexed universal policies you can use the overfunded amount to supplement your retirement income. You could even use that for college funding for your kids or grand kids.

These days there is also something called a terminal or critical illness rider on there. This means you can withdraw a certain percentage of your death benefit amount prior to dying if you are diagnosed with a terminal illness. For instance you have a $500,000 policy and you're diagnosed with terminal cancer and only have a year to live. If you want to pull out $100,000 because you want to enjoy your last moments on earth, you can go ahead and do that. If you do this, when you die, there's only $400,000 left in your death benefit that your beneficiaries will get because they've already given you $100,000.

There's also a long term care rider on there. If you have some kind of long term care event and you cannot perform at least 2 of the 6 ADLs, you can use up to 2% of the value of the death benefit. This can be done on a monthly basis to pay for a nursing home or home health care where a nurse is coming in or someone is taking care of you. Remember that a doctor does have to diagnose it and tell the insurance company that you cannot perform 2 out of the 6 ADLs. These riders are typically paid out indemnity style. You will recall that means that they will give you the check and you do what you want with that check. You don't have to pay for it up front and get reimbursed. You don't have to show them; see I'm in the nursing home, here's my bill. Nope. They just give it to you, tax free. It's also international, typically. This means that if you find out that there's an experimental procedure in Europe somewhere you can go ahead and have that procedure done and it will be covered.

In another type of life insurance called survivorship a married couple would get a policy that is insuring both lives. Most people would think "If my spouse dies, I get the benefit." No. It only pays out on the second death. If the husband dies and 5 years later the wife dies, it would be paid out after the wife dies. Many people typically do this to prevent a tax burden on their kids or grandkids. This is a great vehicle if you have a sizable estate.

So far we have been talking about individual policies but there are also group life insurance policies available. These are typically obtained at work and the employer is paying for the premiums for all the employees. One of the potential problems with group life insurance policies is that they're not usually portable. When you leave that company whether it be because you get fired, resign or retire that life insurance coverage goes away and you don't have that $10-50,000 life insurance policy anymore. Because of this even if you have group life insurance you should have your own personal policy as well. That way you don't have to worry about anything happening in the event that you leave the company or stop working. You can see that Life Insurance has changed tremendously over the years. Remember that you should always consult your tax professional; either a CPA or your accountant to discuss any tax implications. Because if it's structured right there can be a lot of tax advantages.

So, what's next? I'll reveal that in the next chapter.

Don't forget to visit unvarnishedtruthbook.com for more information and your free reports.

Notes

Chapter 10
Summary
"So now what?"

Now that you have been educated about the different types of policies that are out there and what to look out for within these policies and what's important to have in there, the next step is getting the right advisor or agent. There are a lot of different people who call themselves advisors or "financial advisors". Just because they have a license doesn't necessarily mean that they're qualified. The big thing you have to find out is what is their agenda? What is their philosophy as far as business is concerned? Are they more concerned about their commission and how much money they're going to make off of you or do they truly want to work for you and put your best interests at heart? Many times I will tell both my current clients and my prospective clients to not go with the products I have and stay where they're at because that's in their best interest because what I have may not be suitable for them. And it's always amazing to me how they are surprised at that. I've heard time and time again; "Wow I've never heard that before, that's why I like working with you, Glen".

What are the qualifications of a good advisor or agent and how can you tell if someone is qualified or even licensed? In order to sell insurance you have to have a license in the state that you reside in. The easiest way to check on your agent is go to the NIPR website at www.nipr.com. There you can look up their name and it will show you whether or not they're licensed. It is important for you to do this because anyone could say "Oh, yeah, I'm licensed." But I've seen in my 10 years of experience that there are people out there that are giving financial advice, advice on insurance and "educating" clients on insurance and they don't even have a license. So what do they do when someone wants to purchase a policy from them? They write the insurance under someone that they know; whether it be a spouse or girlfriend or whatever. I've heard them say; "Well, I want to help out my (insert relationship here)." You really do have to be careful about that.

It is also possible to obtain a producer's license in other states that you don't reside in. That's called a non-resident license. For example, I have my resident license in Illinois, because that's where I live. I also have a non-resident license in Wisconsin, Michigan, and Alabama. Because those are all states in which I have clients. What that means is I can write policies for them.

Obviously face-to-face is my preferred method, but there are times where I'll either call them on the phone or maybe Skype with them or do a video conference. But never will I take an application without seeing them physically write and sign the application, what's called a wet signature. However are times where you can do what's called an electronic signature. .Going back to that example of having a video conference, everything is submitted online and then the application is sent electronically to the applicant. They look it over, e-sign it and then it is sent to me. I then e-sign it and submit the electronic paperwork and signatures to the insurance provider. All of this is legal, ethical and moral.

In my opinion there are three ways to do business: there's the right and legal way of doing it, where you follow all the rules and regulations and laws of not only the state but also the federal government. Then there's the gray area where it's not illegal, buuut they won't know, so we're going to bend the rules a little bit. And then of course there's the illegal side of it where they'll do whatever it takes just to make money, more often than not. You want to work with someone who's going to not only do things legally, but promote and conduct their business legally, ethically and morally as well. In other words you want to work with someone who stays out of that "gray area". Unfortunately, I've seen circumstances where other agents perform their business in all three areas.

If you're sitting down with an insurance agent, ask them, "Do you have your insurance license?" Chances are they'll say yes, if they're smart. Ask them to show you their license, because technically, at least in the state of Illinois, you have to carry proof that you are licensed. In my opinion if they can't produce that proof then you shouldn't be to be working with that person. Since we are now in the digital age, it can be an electronic copy on their computer or on their phone. There is absolutely no excuse now for someone not to have those kinds of credentials with them.

When someone is talking about the more complex investments like stocks, bonds, mutual funds, and the variable versions of annuities and life insurance they have to be securities licensed. With securities licensing you become a registered representative with FINRA and are under a lot of scrutiny. Typically they start out with a Series 6 license, then series 63, and some get a series 65 license. These agents are able to advise people and sell products like mutual funds, variable annuities, and variable life insurance products.

When someone gets a series 7 license, they can advise about and sell stocks. You can check to make sure your advisor is securities licensed, how long they've held their license, what series they have, what companies they work for and whether or not there are any complaints against them. In order to do this, go to www.finra.org and look them up by clicking on the link that says 'find an agent' or 'find a registered representative' and their profile will come up. Based on the results you can really make an educated decision as to whether or not this is the kind of person you want to work with. I would personally not want to work with someone who's lost their license or even had complaints against them.

Just because an "advisor" is not securities licensed doesn't make them a bad advisor. That just means that they don't sell the variable products or the mutual funds, stocks and bonds. That's all. Maybe, like me, their main focus is protecting the assets of their clients through insurance products and they have built a team of securities licensed advisors that they can refer this type of business to. And that's not necessarily a bad thing.

Another way of determining whether an agent or advisor is someone of character that you would want to work with is by asking the people in your community, or friends or family that are working with this agent or advisor. You may encounter an advisor or agent that has designations such as LUCTF or CFP (Certified Financial Planner) after their name. Designations don't necessarily mean they are "better". It does mean that they are better educated, and they may be more qualified because they've gone through even more classes to get that specialized training. Just because someone does not have those letters behind their name doesn't mean that they're not qualified. It just means that perhaps they have a different philosophy. It takes some time to achieve those designations, maybe even a year or two. If it concerns you, you could ask your advisor why they don't have any letters or certifications when someone else does. Then see what they say. Maybe they're in the process of taking the classes. I know I'm always looking for opportunities to educate myself so I can be a better advisor and coach for my clients.

Another mark of a good advisor/agent is whether they have yearly reviews. You should always review all of your insurance policies whether it be your home owners, auto insurance, everything, with your insurance agent at least once a year because things change. I like to have at least a phone call once a quarter with each of my client, but at the very least you should be offered a yearly review. There are some clients that don't want my review. But they are going to receive a phone call from me, making sure that nothing has happened, and see if anything has changed, because I want to make sure that they are in the right product and they, their family and their assets are fully protected.

My hope is that this book has been beneficial to you and has educated you on what to look out for in your policies and your advisor as well. For a free analysis you can email me at myinsuranceguyglen@gmail.com or go to the website unvarnishedtruthbook.com for free reports as well as a list of A rated companies. That's yet another thing; you should always work with a company that is at least A rated. If it's B rated or lower that means that the company may not be as financially stable as an A rated company due to their assets and financial reserves.

Feel free to sign up for a free Financial Needs Analysis or the newsletter by visiting unvarnishedtruthbook.com.

Notes

Notes